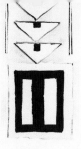

SACAGAWEA

by **Lise Erdrich**

artwork by **Julie Buffalohead**

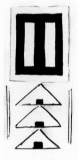

❧ Carolrhoda Books/Minneapolis

For my nieces and nephews —L.E.
For my parents, Roger and Priscilla —J.B.

The publisher would like to thank Dr. Mary Jane Schneider,
Chair of the Department of Indian Studies at the University of North Dakota,
for her assistance in the preparation of this book.

Text copyright © 2003 by Lise Erdrich
Illustrations copyright © 2003 by Julie Buffalohead
Map by Laura Westlund

Carolrhoda Books
A division of Lerner Publishing Group, Inc.
241 First Avenue North
Minneapolis, MN 55401 USA

For reading levels and more information, look up this title at www.lernerbooks.com.

Library of Congress Cataloging-in-Publication Data

Erdrich, Liselotte.
Sacagawea / by Lise Erdrich ; illustrations by Julie Buffalohead.
p. cm.
Summary: A biography of the Shoshone girl Sacagawea from age eleven when she was kidnapped by the Hitdatsa to the end of her journey with Lewis and Clark, plus speculation about her later life.
Includes bibliographical references.
ISBN 978-0-87614-646-0 (lib. bdg. : alk. paper)
ISBN 978-1-5705-679-1 (EB pdf
1. Sacagawea—Juvenile literature. 2. Shoshoni women—Biography—Juvenile literature. 3. Shoshoni Indians—Biography—Juvenile literature. 4. Lewis and Clark Expedition (1804–1806)—Juvenile literature. [1. Sacagawea. 2. Shoshoni Indians—Biography. 3. Indians of North America—Biography. 4. Women—Biography. 5. Lewis and Clark Expedition (1804–1806)] I. Buffalohead, Julie, ill. II. Title.
F592.7.S123 E73 2003
978.004'9745'0092—dc21
2002012504

Manufactured in the United States of America
9-47354-6746-3/4/2019

Author's Note

People disagree about the spelling and pronunciation of the name of the teenage girl who traveled with Lewis and Clark and the Corps of Discovery.

Native American tribes had no written language at the time of the expedition. Even educated American men, such as Captain Lewis, often spelled words by ear or in an irregular fashion. So even the journals from the expedition do not tell us how the young girl's name was spelled.

The official spelling chosen by the state of North Dakota is "Sakakawea." Language experts agree that this version is most true to the Hidatsa words for Bird Woman: *tsakaka*, meaning bird, and *wias*, meaning woman. This spelling is also approved by the Three Affiliated Tribes of North Dakota. There is no soft g sound in the Hidatsa language, so the name would have sounded more like sa-KA-ga-WEE-ah than SA-ka-ja-WEE-ah.

"Sacagawea" is the official spelling used by the U.S. Board on Geographic Names, the U.S. National Park Service, the National Geographic Society, and the U.S. Mint. This seems to be a suitable compromise.

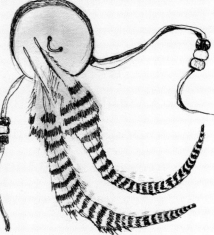

IN A ROCKY MOUNTAIN VALLEY where three rivers flowed into one, near the year 1800, a group of Shoshone Indians had set up camp. They came down out of the mountains only once a year in search of buffalo. On this day, the women were drying buffalo meat over the fire and the men had gone hunting. A young girl, about eleven or twelve years old, was busy helping to prepare for winter. She gathered roots and berries and firewood along the riverbank. The women had to work quickly. They were in enemy territory, and the enemy tribes had rifles.

Suddenly, the tipi camp exploded
in noise and confusion. The
enemy was attacking! The girl ran
into the river, trying to escape.
Hidatsa warriors grabbed her and
sped away on horseback. Other
Shoshone were captured or killed.
Their beautiful horses were stolen.

THE HIDATSA WARRIORS and their captives traveled east. Mountains and forests faded in the distance behind them as they crossed the Great Plains. The young Shoshone girl was overwhelmed by the vast open space as she was taken farther and farther from all she knew.

She stared in astonishment when at last, one morning, they reached the earth lodge villages of the Hidatsa and Mandan people. Women were paddling down a river in bowl-shaped boats on the way to their gardens. Smoke rose from large upside-down bowls crowded on the high riverbank. These bowls had doors with people coming out. So many!

There were five thousand people in the Indian villages where the Knife River entered the Missouri River. Even St. Louis, the important far-off city of white man fur traders, did not have that many people.

THE YOUNG SHOSHONE GIRL joined a Hidatsa household. She was given the name Sacagawea, which means "Bird Woman." The Hidatsa women taught her how to tend their gardens, which grew in the rich soil along the river. Sacagawea marveled at the wonderful new plants—corn, squash, beans, pumpkins, sunflowers. Her Shoshone people did not grow gardens. They were wanderers who gathered their food from the wild.

Sacagawea learned to sing to the corn to help it grow. She chased away hungry birds. The sunflower, friendly soul of the garden, brightened her days. She carried home the harvest in a round bullboat, a boat made from a buffalo hide with the tail left on for a handle.

SACAGAWEA had been with the Hidatsa family almost four years when she was given in marriage to Toussaint Charbonneau, a French Canadian fur trapper. Sacagawea was no more than sixteen. Charbonneau was at least twenty years older than she was.

WHILE SACAGAWEA was learning the ways of her new world, President Thomas Jefferson was making plans for an expedition. It would be known as the Corps of Discovery.

The people of the United States knew almost nothing about the land between the Mississippi River and the Pacific Ocean. And the Native Americans who lived there did not know that the United States had just bought a large portion of this land from France. Indeed, they did not believe that any of the earth could be bought or sold.

Jefferson was hoping explorers could find a way to travel most of the way from the Mississippi to the Pacific by boat. He also wanted them to learn everything they could about this unknown land and the people who lived there.

The expedition would be led by Captain Meriwether Lewis and Captain William Clark. It would begin near St. Louis, where the Missouri River flowed into the Mississippi.

On May 14, 1804, a crew of more than forty men set off against the Missouri River current in a keelboat and two large canoes called pirogues. The Corps of Discovery was under way.

THE EXPEDITION arrived at the Knife River villages at the end of October. They were greeted with great excitement. Sacagawea heard tales of a gigantic black dog that traveled with the explorers. She heard that a fierce and awesome "white man" with black skin was among the crew. This was York, the slave of Captain Clark.

The explorers built a fort and called it Fort Mandan. Then they settled in to spend the winter at the Knife River villages. Lewis and Clark soon learned they would need horses to cross the Rocky Mountains. The people of the villages told them they could get the horses from the Shoshone when the expedition reached the mountain passes.

THE WILY CHARBONNEAU proposed
that they hire him as a guide and interpreter.
He did not speak Shoshone, but Sacagawea did.
He told her they would be joining the Corps of
Discovery in the spring. This was exciting
news, but Sacagawea's mind was on other
matters. She was soon to become a mother.

IN FEBRUARY, the time came for Sacagawea to have her baby. It was a long, difficult birth. Captain Lewis wanted to help her. He gave a crew member two rattlesnake rattles to crush and mix with water. Just a few minutes after drinking the mixture, Sacagawea gave birth to a baby boy. He was named Jean-Baptiste Charbonneau, but Captain Clark called him Pompy. Before long, the boy was known to everyone as Pomp.

On April 7, 1805, the Corps of Discovery started west, struggling upstream on the mighty, muddy Missouri in two pirogues and six smaller canoes. Pomp was not yet two months old. As Sacagawea walked along the riverbank, she carried Pomp on her back, in a cradleboard or wrapped up snug in her shawl.

EVERY MEMBER of the Corps of Discovery was hired for a special skill— hunter, blacksmith, woodsman, sailor. As an interpreter, Charbonneau was paid much more than the other crew members. But his skills as a sailor, guide, and outdoorsman were very poor. The only thing he did well was cook buffalo sausage.

Sacagawea did what she could to help the expedition, even though she was paid nothing. As she walked along the shore with Captain Clark, Sacagawea looked for plants to keep the crew healthy. She gathered berries or dug for wild artichoke roots with her digging stick. Her Shoshone childhood had prepared her well for this journey.

THE CORPS had been traveling less than two months when near disaster struck. Charbonneau was steering a boat through choppy waters when a sudden high wind tipped it sideways. He lost his wits and dropped the rudder while the boat filled with water. The expedition's valuables were spilling overboard! Charbonneau was ordered to right the boat or be shot.

Sacagawea stayed calm and rescued the captains' important things—journals, gunpowder, medicines, scientific instruments—every bundle she could reach. Without these supplies, the expedition could not have continued.

A few days later, they came to a beautiful river. The grateful captains named it after Sacagawea.

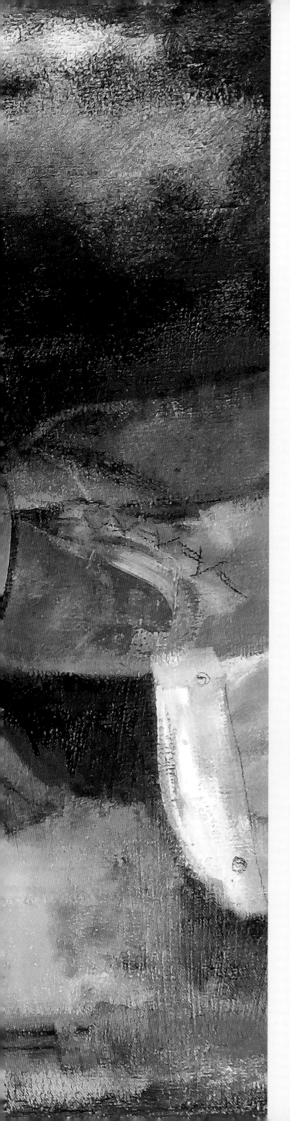

By June, the Corps was entering mountain country. Soon they could hear the distant roaring sound of the Great Falls of the Missouri. Captain Lewis thought the waterfall was the grandest sight he had ever seen. But there was no way to get past it by boat. It would take the corps nearly a month to get around the Great Falls and the four waterfalls they found just beyond it.

The crew built creaky, clumsy wagons to carry their boats and supplies. Battered by hail, rain, and wind, the men dragged the wagons over sharp rocks and prickly pear cactus that punctured their moccasins.

One day, a freak cloudburst caused a flash flood. Rocks, mud, and water came crashing down the canyon. Sacagawea held on to her son as tight as she could while Clark pushed and pulled them both to safety. Pomp's cradleboard, clothes, and bedding were swept away by the rushing water, but all three were unharmed.

BY THE MIDDLE OF JULY, the corps was once again paddling up the Missouri. They reached a valley where three rivers came together, a place Sacagawea knew well. If she was upset to see it again, she did not show it. The captains learned how Sacagawea had been captured and her people killed.

Sacagawea recognized a landmark that her people called the Beaver Head Mountain. She knew they must be nearing the summer camp of the Shoshone.

Nearly two weeks later, Sacagawea walked along the river, scanning the familiar territory. She spotted some men on horseback far ahead of them. Suddenly, Captain Clark saw Sacagawea dance up and down with happiness, sucking her fingers. He knew this sign meant that these were her people, the Shoshone.

An excited crowd greeted the explorers at the Shoshone camp. Although years had passed since Sacagawea had been captured, a Shoshone woman recognized her. She rushed up to Sacagawea and threw her arms around her.

LEWIS AND CLARK had discovered that their need for Shoshone horses was even greater than they thought. There was far more mountain country between the Missouri River and a water route to the Pacific than they expected. A grand council was called to discuss the matter. Sacagawea was to be one of the translators.

Interpreting for the men at the chief's council was a serious responsibility. Sacagawea wanted to do her best. But when she looked at the face of the Shoshone chief, she burst into tears. He was her brother, Cameahwait! Sacagawea jumped up, threw her blanket over her brother, and wept.

Cameahwait was moved, too. But the council had to continue. Though tears kept flooding back, Sacagawea kept to her duty until the council ended.

SACAGAWEA spent the last days of August with her people. The time passed too quickly. Before long, the expedition had to mount Shoshone horses and continue across the mountains, leaving their boats behind.

The next part of their journey almost killed them. The mountain paths were narrow and dangerous, especially once it started to snow. Their feet froze, they didn't have enough to eat, and the mountains seemed without end.

Finally, the expedition emerged on the Pacific side of the Rockies. There Nez Perce Indians helped them make new boats and agreed to keep the horses in case they returned that way in the spring.

With great relief, the crew dropped their boats into the Clearwater River and let the current carry the expedition toward the ocean.

AT THE BEGINNING of November, the explorers noticed a sound that could only be the crashing of waves. They had finally reached the Pacific Ocean!

The crew voted on where to make winter camp. Sacagawea was allowed to vote, too. She wanted to stay where she could find plenty of wapato roots for winter food. They set up camp not far from the ocean, in case a ship came to take them back home. But by now, people back east were sure the whole corps was long dead. No ship came for them.

A cold rain soaked the crew as they cut logs and built Fort Clatsop. The hunters went to find game, while Sacagawea dug for wapato roots in the soggy ground.

Christmas Day was rainy and dreary, but the corps was determined to celebrate. The men fired a salute with their guns and sang. Sacagawea gave Captain Clark a fine gift of two dozen white weasel tails.

IN EARLY JANUARY, Clark heard from some Indians that a whale had washed up onshore. He decided to go to the ocean to get blubber for the crew to eat. They were tired of their diet of lean spoiled meat and fish.

Sacagawea gathered up her courage and insisted that she be allowed to accompany Clark. She hadn't traveled so far to leave without ever seeing the ocean! And she wanted to see that monstrous creature. The captains agreed to let her go.

At last, Sacagawea saw the Pacific Ocean. She stood and stared at the great waters stretching endlessly in front of her. On the beach was the great skeleton of the whale. It was an amazing sight, nearly as long as twenty men lying end to end. The whale had been picked clean, but Clark was able to buy some blubber from the Indians to feed his men.

THE CREW STAYED BUSY all winter,
hunting, sewing moccasins, and making repairs on their
equipment. Clark made maps, while Lewis worked on his
report to President Jefferson.

    Sacagawea watched over Pomp as he began to walk.
Captain Clark called him "my little dancing boy." He had
become very attached to Sacagawea and her son. When the
time came, it would be hard for them to part.

SPRING ARRIVED, and it was time to go back the way they had come. In late March, the Corps of Discovery headed up the Columbia River to retrieve their horses from the Nez Perce.

At a place called Traveler's Rest, the expedition divided into two groups. Sacagawea would help guide Clark's group south to the Yellowstone River. Lewis's group would head northeast to explore the Marias River.

At the end of July, Clark's group came across an enormous rock tower on the banks of the Yellowstone. Clark named it Pompy's Tower in honor of his beloved little friend. In the side of the rock, he carved:

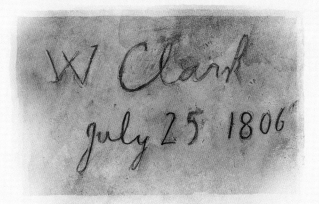

THE TWO GROUPS MET up on August 12. Two days later, Sacagawea gazed once again upon the round earth lodges of the Knife River villages. She had been gone a year and four months.

Lewis and Clark prepared to return to St. Louis. Before they left, Captain Clark came to talk to Sacagawea and Charbonneau. He offered to take Pomp back to St. Louis with him. He would see that the boy had a good education and would raise him as his own son.

Sacagawea knew that Captain Clark would take good care of her child. But he was not even two years old. She couldn't let him go yet. Sacagawea and Charbonneau promised they would bring Pomp to visit Clark in a year or so.

ON AUGUST 17, 1806, Sacagawea watched as the
Corps of Discovery set off again down the Missouri
River. Her journey of exploration was over, but the
Corps of Discovery still had hundreds of miles to go.

Afterword

When the Corps of Discovery returned to St. Louis, they were greeted with cheers and celebrations. News of the expedition's success spread quickly. Lewis and Clark were known across the United States as heroes.

Sacagawea's story is not as easy to follow. When Pomp was about five years old, Sacagawea and Charbonneau took him to St. Louis and left him with Captain Clark. Clark sent Pomp to boarding school to learn to read and write, and about the ways of white society.

It is believed that Sacagawea gave birth to a daughter named Lizette in the summer of 1812. In the winter of that same year, there were reports that Charbonneau's young wife died of a fever at Fort Manuel in what would become South Dakota. Most historians think that the woman who died was Sacagawea. But some think it was Charbonneau's other Shoshone wife who died that winter.

Some people believe Sacagawea lived to be an old woman. According to Shoshone legend, a woman called Sacajawea died in 1884 on the Wind River Indian Reservation in Wyoming. She was nearly one hundred years old. A North Dakota legend says that a Hidatsa woman named Sakakawea, who was in her eighties, was killed by an enemy war party in Montana in 1869.

Whether or not Sacagawea survived to old age, people will always remember her as a brave young girl with a baby peeking over her shoulder. When she set off up the Missouri River with the Corps of Discovery, she could not have known that she would become a legend.

Fort Clatsop

Marias R.

Lewis's return route

Traveler's Rest

Missouri R.

Great Falls

Clearwater R.

Columbia R.

Three Forks

Sacagawea R.

Clark's return route

Pompy's Tower

Shoshone camp

Yellowstone R.

Miles

| 0 | 100 | 200 |

| 0 | 100 | 200 | 300 |
Kilometers

Timeline

about 1789	Sacagawea is born, probably in present-day Idaho.
about 1800	Sacagawea is captured by Hidatsa warriors in present-day Montana.
about 1803	Sacagawea is given in marriage to Toussaint Charbonneau.
1803	The $15 million Louisiana Purchase adds a vast western territory to the United States.
May 1804	The Corps of Discovery sets off from Camp Wood near St. Louis on May 14.
October 1804	The expedition reaches the Knife River villages in present-day North Dakota.
November 1804	The expedition builds Fort Mandan.
February 1805	Jean-Baptiste Charbonneau, known as Pomp, is born to Sacagawea and Charbonneau on February 11.
April 1805	The Corps of Discovery leaves the Knife River villages and heads west on April 7.
May 1805	Sacagawea rescues the expedition's supplies. The captains name a river after her.
June 1805	The expedition reaches the Great Falls of the Missouri River in present-day Montana.
July 1805	The expedition reaches the Three Forks of the Missouri River, site of Sacagawea's kidnapping about five years earlier.
August 1805	Sacagawea is reunited with her Shoshone people and recognizes her brother, Cameahwait.
November 1805	The expedition sets up camp near the Pacific Ocean.
December 1805	The expedition builds Fort Clatsop.
January 1806	Sacagawea sees the Pacific Ocean for the first time.
March 1806	The Corps of Discovery sets off for home.
July 1806	Clark names a rock formation in present-day Montana Pompy's Tower (later called Pompey's Pillar) after Pomp.

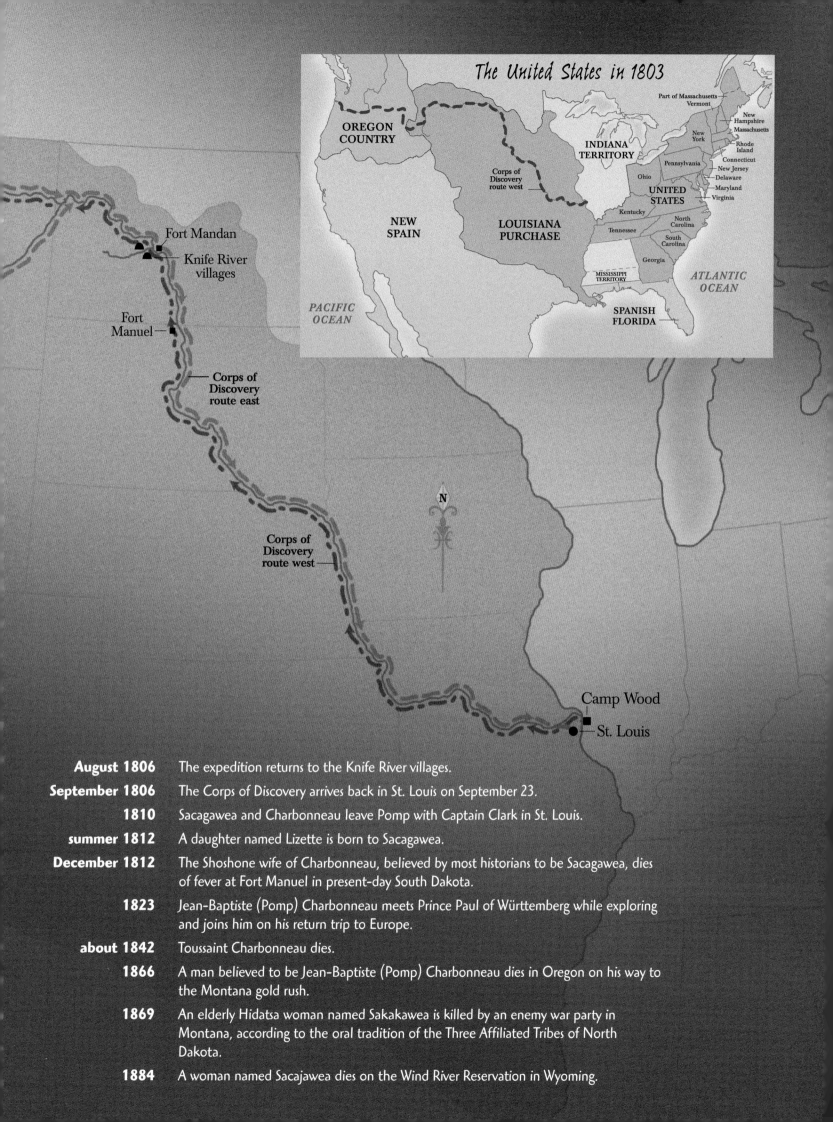

The United States in 1803

OREGON COUNTRY

INDIANA TERRITORY

Corps of Discovery route west

NEW SPAIN

LOUISIANA PURCHASE

UNITED STATES

Kentucky

Tennessee

North Carolina

South Carolina

Georgia

Ohio

Pennsylvania

New York

Vermont

Part of Massachusetts

New Hampshire

Massachusetts

Rhode Island

Connecticut

New Jersey

Delaware

Maryland

Virginia

MISSISSIPPI TERRITORY

SPANISH FLORIDA

PACIFIC OCEAN

ATLANTIC OCEAN

Fort Mandan

Knife River villages

Fort Manuel

Corps of Discovery route east

N

Corps of Discovery route west

Camp Wood

St. Louis

August 1806	The expedition returns to the Knife River villages.
September 1806	The Corps of Discovery arrives back in St. Louis on September 23.
1810	Sacagawea and Charbonneau leave Pomp with Captain Clark in St. Louis.
summer 1812	A daughter named Lizette is born to Sacagawea.
December 1812	The Shoshone wife of Charbonneau, believed by most historians to be Sacagawea, dies of fever at Fort Manuel in present-day South Dakota.
1823	Jean-Baptiste (Pomp) Charbonneau meets Prince Paul of Württemberg while exploring and joins him on his return trip to Europe.
about 1842	Toussaint Charbonneau dies.
1866	A man believed to be Jean-Baptiste (Pomp) Charbonneau dies in Oregon on his way to the Montana gold rush.
1869	An elderly Hidatsa woman named Sakakawea is killed by an enemy war party in Montana, according to the oral tradition of the Three Affiliated Tribes of North Dakota.
1884	A woman named Sacajawea dies on the Wind River Reservation in Wyoming.

Select Bibliography

De Voto, Barnard, ed., *The Journals of Lewis and Clark*. Boston: Houghton Mifflin, 1953.

Gilman, Carolyn, and Mary Jane Schneider. *The Way to Independence: Memories of a Hidatsa Indian Family, 1840–1920*. St. Paul, MN: Minnesota Historical Society Press, 1987.

Reid, Russell. *Sakakawea: The Bird Woman*. Bismarck, ND: State Historical Society of North Dakota, 1986.

Rogers, Ken. "Sakakawea and the Fur Traders." Special to the *Bismarck Tribune*, 1998.

Wilson, Gilbert L. *Buffalo Bird Woman's Garden*. 1917. Reprint, St. Paul, MN: Minnesota Historical Society Press, 1987.

Wilson, Gilbert L. *Waheenee: An Indian Girl's Story*. 1921. Reprint, Lincoln, NE: University of Nebraska Press, 1981.